I0111885

AltStrings Fiddle Method

FOR VIOLIN

Book 1

Original Key

Second Edition

Caroline McCaskey

Music Arranged by Caroline McCaskey

Cover Design: Mary Margaret McMurtry
www.marymcmurtrydesign.com

Cover Art and Illustrations: Jessica Blackburn, Blackburn Renderings
www.blackburnrenderings.com

Graphic Layout and Music Engraving: Charylu Roberts, O.Ruby Productions
www.selfpublishmusicbooks.com

ISBN 978-1-952077-00-5

Table of Contents

Songs

For additional multimedia content including video lessons on each tune and technique, point the camera on your mobile device at the QR codes found throughout the book, or follow the links to *altstrings.com*.

Thank You for Choosing the AltStrings Fiddle Method!

There are two purposes to this series:

1. To provide the student with an introduction to playing North American and Celtic instrumental folk music, including adding ornamentation, playing backup chords and rhythms, and creating twin fiddle parts and other harmonies. This book can be used on its own (with a qualified teacher to introduce new concepts), or as a supplement to classical study.

2. To offer a pedagogically appropriate resource for supplemental study to any of the mainstream teaching methods, aiming to be useful to both students and teachers regardless of prior experience or training in playing traditional music. My hope is that this method is helpful to both teachers and students, whether they have a strong traditional music background or are just beginning their non-classical journey.

TUNE	KEY	SKILLS
1. Twinkle, Twinkle Little Star	A	"Down little Up little" bowing, drone string
2. Mary Had a Little Lamb	A	Scale motion, "tunnel" second finger over E string
3. Goodbye Liza Jane	A	Scale motion and rapid string crossings
4. Highland Laddie	A	Introduces D string
5. Kerry Polka	D	Rapid string crossings with many open strings
6. Cripple Creek	A	Can be used to teach or reinforce A Major arpeggio
7. Rubber Dolly	A	Long notes (opportunity to save bow), significant D string usage
8. Moneymusk	A	Steady eighth notes, four-note patterns
9. Old Joe Clark	A mix	Introduces low second finger
10. Peek-A-Boo Waltz	D	Longer melody, use of low second finger
11. Cluck Old Hen	A mix/a min	Introduces slides, to both C sharp and C natural
12. Skye Boat Song	G	Introduces hooked bowing and slurs
13. La Bastringue	D	C sharp vs. C natural, arpeggiation
14. Soldier's Joy	D	Reinforces D Major arpeggio
15. Sweet Betsy from Pike	G	Can be used to teach or reinforce G Major arpeggio
16. Love Somebody	D	Hooked bowing (up bows on two repeated notes)
17. Red Haired Boy	D	Slurring groups of two eighth notes
18. Row Your Boat	G	Hooked bowing (down bows and up bows)
19. Pop Goes the Weasel	G	Hooked bowing, left hand pizzicato
20. Off She Goes	D	Complex finger patterns

Posture

How to Hold the Fiddle

When you stand to play, your feet should be shoulder-width apart, with your weight balanced evenly on each foot.

If you are sitting to play (in a group, for example), make sure your feet are balanced as if you were standing. Be sure to sit on the edge of your chair.

Don't reach for the fiddle with your head and neck—bring your fiddle to you!

The fiddle sits on your left shoulder, with the end button touching your neck. Try using a shoulder rest or a sponge underneath the instrument to make it more stable.

The weight of your head is enough to hold the instrument—don't squeeze.

Place your left hand thumbprint on the fiddle neck, and the side of your pointer finger, just above the knuckle, across the neck from your thumb. On most fiddles, this is right about where the neck changes color. Some teachers like the thumb to be a little farther forward, and that's okay too. Don't squeeze! There should be a little triangle of space under the fiddle neck, between your thumb and your hand.

Your left wrist needs to be straight—no serving pizza! Your left elbow should hang straight down; use your head to hold the instrument, not your hand.

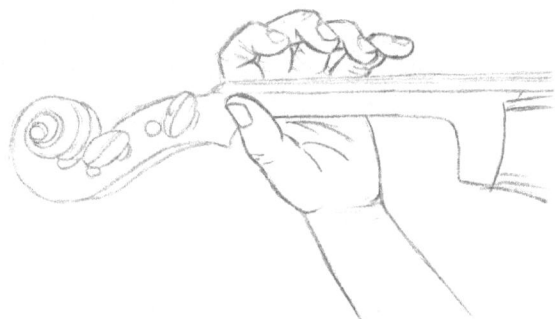

How to Hold the Bow

Hold your bow near the middle of the stick in your left hand. Be careful not to touch the hair!

Flop your right hand fingers over the top of the bow at the frog. They should be relaxed with some space in between each one.

Bend your thumb and put the corner of your thumb nail under the frog, at the very edge of the silver part. You can put a sticker or corn bandage there to remind you where it goes.

Note: many teachers like to start beginners with their thumbs under the frog, because it keeps your hand open and relaxed. Once you are very comfortable with your bow hold (and have no straight fingers or thumb) you can move your thumb inside the frog. Be sure and wait until your teacher says it's okay!

Your pinky bends and rests on top of and slightly behind the bow stick, right on the tip of your fingernail. You can wrap a rubber band or a pencil grip around the bow stick to help keep it from sliding off.

Point the tip of the bow up to the ceiling. This lets you practice your bow hold without getting tired and squeezing your fingers.

If your pinky won't stay bent, you may be putting weight on it. Try tapping your pinky, which makes the other fingers do the work of supporting the bow instead.

Putting it All Together

Make sure you can hold the bow on its own before you add it to the fiddle!

Check your bow in the mirror to make sure it is parallel to the bridge. It will look strange up close to your face, so use the mirror to help you learn what it should look and feel like.

Find the spot where your arm makes a right angle. You can put a sticker on your bow to help you remember where it is.

Hold your upper arm still – you should open and close your elbow to move your forearm and hand only. From your right angle bow position, you can open your elbow for a down bow, and the bow should stay fairly straight.

Try some open string rhythms to make sure you are playing with a straight bow.

How to Use Your Fingers

Just like on your bow hand, your left hand fingers should be floppy with a little bit of space between each one.

Since the violin doesn't have any frets to help you figure out where your fingers go, you can put tape on the fingerboard under the strings to help you aim. Some companies manufacture pre-cut tape especially for this purpose, or you can use masking tape or car striping tape instead. You may want to ask your teacher to help, to make sure they go in the right place.

Make sure you are playing with rounded fingers, with both joints bent. Your fingers should touch the strings on their fingertips, on the side of the tip closer to your thumb. Don't worry if your pinky is only bent a little bit — it's short, so that's ok. Don't lift your hand too high in order to accommodate the pinky (for example, don't have your knuckle above the fingerboard).

Pre-Flight Checklist

Just as a pilot checks his plane before takeoff, you should check your setup EVERY TIME before you play, until doing it the right way becomes the easy way.

Don't give up! It seems like a long list, but if you prepare carefully, it will quickly become muscle memory.

Here is your checklist:

General

- Feet shoulder-width apart and weight balanced evenly
- Fiddle sits on your left shoulder with the end button touching your neck
- Hold the fiddle with your head, not your hands, and don't squeeze

Left Hand

- Thumbprint and side of index finger in the same place every time
- Straight wrist, elbow hangs straight down
- Fingers floppy and hovering above strings ready to play

Bow Hand

- Floppy fingers
- Bent thumb
- Bent pinky

Twinkle, Twinkle Little Star

History

This popular French lullaby has been used many times as the theme for a set of variations, including by Wolfgang Amadeus Mozart and Dr. Shinichi Suzuki.

Performance Notes

To play both strings at once, simply raise or lower your bow arm so that the bow is touching both strings. Make a tunnel with your fingers over the "drone string" (this means the open string played against the notes of the tune. Which string is your drone string?)

Be sure not to touch the open string with your fingers, or it won't ring properly!

*altstrings.com/
violin-fiddle-bk1-1*

Mary Had a Little Lamb

Lyrics

Mary had a little lamb,
Little lamb, little lamb,
Mary had a little lamb whose
Fleece was white as snow.

Everywhere that Mary went,
Mary went, Mary went,
Everywhere that Mary went,
The lamb was sure to go.

History

Originally from England, this song is now sung by children in English-speaking countries around the world.

Performance Notes

Try to leave your second finger down on the A string while you play E in bar 4; you'll need it again in bar 5!

altstrings.com/
violin-fiddle-bk1-2

Goodbye Liza Jane

Lyrics

1. Swing your Ma, Swing your Pa,
   Goodbye, goodbye,
   Swing the girl from Arkansas,
   Goodbye Liza Jane.

2. Oh, how I loved her,
   Ain't that a shame?
   Oh, how I loved her,
   Goodbye Liza Jane.

History

A version of this song was collected by an African-American song collector named Thomas Talley in 1922.

Performance Notes

In bars 10 and 14, use only your second finger – try not to put down your first finger as well.

altstrings.com/
violin-fiddle-bk1-3

Highland Laddie

History

This march has been used by Commonwealth military forces since the 1880s, and is still used by some regiments today. The tune also has a specific dance that goes along with it, as well as several sets of lyrics.

Performance Notes

This is our first tune that includes the D string. You can raise your bow hand and elbow to tip your bow to the D string, but be sure not to raise your right shoulder. You can also bring your left elbow forward to help your fingers reach the D string, and don't forget to lower it again for the A and E strings.

This is good fiddle technique!

altstrings.com/
violin-fiddle-bk1-4

Kerry Polka

History

A polka is a type of dance from Bohemia, which is now part of the Czech Republic. The polka was introduced to Ireland in the late 19th century. Today there are hundreds of Irish polkas, which are played on the fiddle or button accordion.

Performance Notes

In bars 3 and 11, use only your third finger—try not to put down your first and second fingers as well.

altstrings.com/
violin-fiddle-bk1-5

11

Cripple Creek

Lyrics

Goin' up to Cripple Creek, goin' on a run,
Goin' up to Cripple Creek to have a little fun.
Goin' up to Cripple Creek, goin' on a whirl,
Goin' up to Cripple Creek to see my girl.

History

This is a folk song from the Appalachian Mountains. The name "Cripple Creek" might either refer to a place in Virginia, or Colorado during the Gold Rush.

Performance Notes

Walking Fingers: Since this tune starts with the third finger, try placing your third finger all by itself at the beginning; this will make it faster to pick up to play the E string. Wrists like to bend when the third finger goes down, so make sure your wrist stays straight! Then, in bar 1 after the E string, try placing your second finger down by itself on the A string. Add your third finger for the next note in bar 2. You can then "walk" to your first finger: place your first finger on the E string, then pick up your second and third fingers, as if your fingers are "walking". This may be tricky at first, but once you can do it, it's a lot faster!

Check out *AltStrings.com* for a video lesson on this technique!

Let's Duet!

Chords symbols are letters (and sometimes other symbols), which are shorthand for a collection of several notes. Let's start with one note at a time — the "root." When you see the letter "A" you can play your open A string, for "D" you can play your D string, and for "E" you can play your E string.

altstrings.com/
violin-fiddle-bk1-6

In the blank spaces, write the previous chord again (and in some cases, again and again), until you reach the next chord. For example, fill in the first blank with an "A."

Ask a friend or your teacher to play the tune, or listen to the recording, while you:

1. Trace your finger along with the music, and say the letter of the chord on each beat.
2. Play one of your open strings on each beat. If the chord symbol says "A," play your A string, etc.

Time Machine

Let's go back in time, and add chords to one of your review tunes. Be sure to check out *AltStrings.com* for help, and practice playing along with the video lessons.

Now that you can play from a chord chart, you can play the tunes you know as duets with your friends!

Goodbye Liza Jane

Rubber Dolly

J. B. Lampe, 1869–1929

Lyrics

My momma told me, if I was goody,
That she would buy me a rubber dolly.
But don't you tell her I got a feller,
'Cuz she won't buy me a rubber dolly.

History

This children's song was once used as a playground song for hand clapping games.

Performance Notes

This is a great tune to practice walking fingers! Every time you have notes going in a down direction without skipping any fingers (you can call this a "descending scale"), you can use walking fingers.

In bar 3, hop your second finger from the D string to the A string, and be sure to drop your left elbow so that you keep a good hand position on each string.

*altstrings.com/
violin-fiddle-bk1-7*

Moneymusk

Copyright © 2020 AltStrings

History

Moneymusk is the name of a town in Scotland. This tune is usually played as a strathspey, a type of tune unique to Scotland. Here, it is arranged as a reel.

Performance Notes

1. Try to stay in the middle of the bow.
2. Open and close your arm to keep the bow straight.
3. To play faster, try using less bow.

Backup Chords

Go back through this tune and write in chords so that there are two chords per bar.
The chords should look like this:

$\frac{4}{4}$ A A | A D | A A | D E :||

||: A A | A A | A A | D E :||

altstrings.com/
violin-fiddle-bk1-8

Ghost/Accent: "Little BIG and" Pattern

Try this in the air first without the bow, or by "soaping" on your arm. (Imagine you have soap on your bow hand, and use up and down bow strokes to pretend to scrub your left arm.) Once it is easy to do that correctly, go ahead and try it on your A string, and then on any other strings you'd like to try. Remember to keep your wrist and fingers loose! The pattern should go like this:

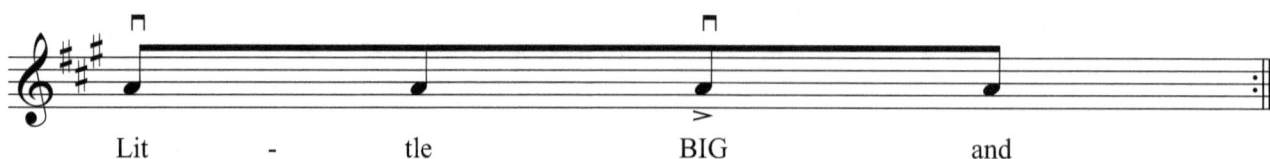

Lit   -   tle   BIG   and

Notes

1. Any accented note should be played with greater bow speed, arm weight and "bite" in the bow hand than the other notes.

2. Any non-accented note should be played with very little bow speed and zero arm weight, and should barely be heard at all. This type of playing is called "ghosting" the bow, and can be used to count with your bow, enabling placement of even very complicated accent patterns.

3. A non-accented note immediately following an accented note can be played with greater bow speed than the other ghosted notes, in order to make up for the amount of bow you used to play your accent. The note should still be played with no arm weight so as not to sound like an accented note.

Once you can do the "Little BIG and" pattern on your open strings, try using it once per chord in our chord progression for "Moneymusk" (there should be two patterns per bar).

Try it as a duet! It should go like this:

Another option is to add your first finger to the D string instead of using open E; this will eliminate the fast string crossings.

Old Joe Clark

Lyrics

Old Joe Clark he had a house,
Fifteen stories high,
Every story in that house was
Filled with chicken pie.

Fare ye well, Old Joe Clark,
Fare ye well I say,
Fare ye well, Old Joe Clark,
I'm a-goin' away.

History

Originally a ballad about a mountaineer, this song has ninety verses!

Performance Notes

Low second finger = next to your first finger
High second finger = next to your third finger (we have used this position until now)

This tune uses a low second finger on the E string (G natural), and a high second finger on the A string (C sharp).

altstrings.com/
violin-fiddle-bk1-9

Peek-A-Boo Waltz

William J. Scanlan, 1856–1898

Lyrics

Peek-a-boo, peek-a-boo,
Come from behind the chair;
Peek-a-boo, peek-a-boo,
I see you hiding there.

History

This fiddle tune was originally a song, and the verse (A part) was in duple meter (2/4) and the chorus (B part) was in waltz time, triple meter, or waltz time (3/4). Today, the whole tune is played as a waltz.

Performance Notes

This tune is full of half notes! Save your bow on the half notes, and also make sure to hold each half note for two beats. That way, people can dance to it!

altstrings.com/
violin-fiddle-bk1-10

Cluck Old Hen

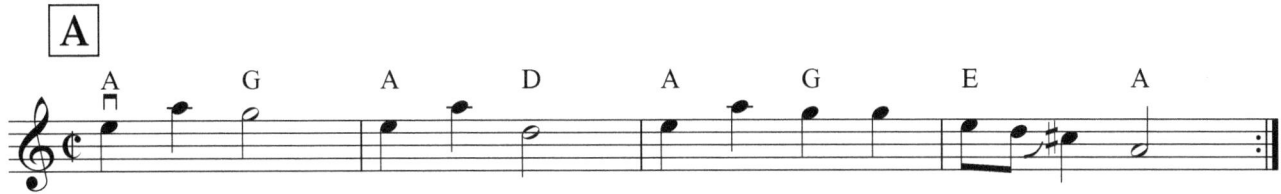

Lyrics

My old hen's a good old hen,
She lays eggs for the railroad men.
Sometimes one, sometimes two,
That's enough for the whole darn crew.

Cluck old hen, cluck and sing,
Ain't laid an egg since way last spring.
Cluck old hen, cluck and squall,
Ain't laid an egg since way last fall.

History

The oldest version of this very old Appalachian song dates back to 1886!

Performance Notes

Slides: In this tune, try sliding your second finger up into position while you bow.
In the A part, you can slide your finger from the low second finger position to the high second finger position.

In the B part, try putting your second finger where your first finger goes, and sliding up to the low second finger position from there.

altstrings.com/
violin-fiddle-bk1-11

Skye Boat Song

Lyrics

Speed bonnie boat like a bird on the wing,
Onward! the sailors cry,
Carry the lad that's born to be king
Over the sea to Skye.

History

This Scottish "lament," or sad song, is about the boat that helped Bonnie Prince Charlie, disguised as an Irish woman, escape from the British army in Scotland to the Isle of Skye.

Performance Notes

Slurs: In bars 1 and 3, each bar gets one long, smooth down bow. It's up to your first finger to change the note!

Hooked bows: In bar 2, those notes are played with hooked bows. Since the notes have lines, separate them with gentle bow strokes.

Form: The *form*, or shape, of this tune is AABBA. These letters tell you how many times to play each part of the tune.

altstrings.com/
violin-fiddle-bk1-12

La Bastringue

13

History

This French Canadian fiddle tune has a specific dance that goes along with it. "La Bastringue" means "the wild party" in French.

Performance Notes

This tune uses a variety of high and low second fingers. On the E string, 2 is always low, and on the A string, sometimes it is high and sometimes it is low. Look for the natural sign to tell you to use a low second finger.

Try learning the harmony, and play along with a friend!

altstrings.com/ violin-fiddle-bk1-13

La Bastringue Harmony

Soldier's Joy

History

This fiddle tune originates from the British Isles, and is now played around the world.

Performance Notes

This tune is played by many different styles of player, from bluegrass to Irish and many more. Try going to a "session" (an informal group of people playing traditional music) and if they ask if you'd like to play a tune, try this one! It is very likely that someone else will know it too, and you can play together.

altstrings.com/
violin-fiddle-bk1-14

Sweet Betsy from Pike

Lyrics

Did you ever hear tell of Sweet Betsy from Pike,
Who crossed the wide mountains with her lover Ike,
With two yoke of cattle, an old yeller dog,
A tall Shanghai rooster and a one-spotted hog?
Singing too-ra-li, oo-ra-li, oo-ra-li-ay.

History

This Gold Rush era folk song by John A. Stone is about a pioneer woman named Betsy, who migrated from Pike County (probably in Missouri) to California.

Performance Notes

Bowing: In many of our previous tunes, most bars have started with a down bow. This is because a down bow works with gravity and the weight of your arm to create an emphasis on a note, and we want to place emphasis on the first beat of the bar. If this didn't occur naturally in the tune, we added slurs or bow lifts to correct it.

This time, we are not going to emphasize on the downbeat of every bar. Instead, we are bowing "as it comes," or alternating down and up strokes, and relying on playing with long, smooth strokes to create a longer phrase. Work with your teacher to figure out which notes could be the most important, and emphasize those notes with your bow. You can do this by using a little bit more bow (moving the bow faster to cover more ground with it) and sinking your arm into the string to give the bow more of the weight from your arm. Try it!

*altstrings.com/
violin-fiddle-bk1-15*

23

Love Somebody

History

This Irish fiddle tune goes by many other names, including "Tripping on the Mountain," "Hair in the Butter" and "Twin Sisters."

Performance Notes

The hooked bows that occur throughout this tune will help you to keep a down bow on the first beat in every bar. Since these notes have dots, play them with shorter bow strokes than you would if they had lines.

Also, try using a fourth finger on A instead of E string on the first note of bar 4.

altstrings.com/
violin-fiddle-bk1-16

Red Haired Boy

History

This tune was originally from Ireland, and went by many other names such as "The Little Beggar Man" and "The Little Red Fox." It is now played throughout Scotland, Ireland, and North America.

Performance Notes

This is a great tune to practice your slurs! Two notes that are slurred together can be practiced first by stopping the bow in between the notes. Once you have mastered that, try playing the notes in the same bow direction, but without stopping the bow.

Please note that in this tune, all of the second fingers on the E string will be low, and all the second fingers on the A string will be high.

altstrings.com/
violin-fiddle-bk1-17

Chords

Now it's time to add another note to our chords. We can already play the "root" of the chord (which is the same as the chord's name). This time we are adding the "fifth" of the chord.

To reach the fifth of the chord, all we have to do is play the next string up. That's it! So, when we see a "D" chord now, we will play both D and A. The same is true for "A"— we'll play both the A and E strings. When we see "G," you guessed it — G and D. It's that simple!

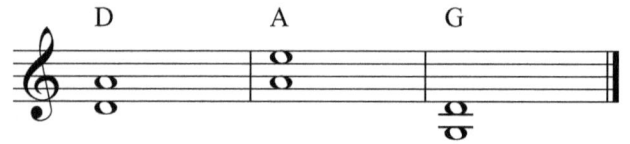

Chopping/Vertical Bowing

Please attempt only under instructor supervision.

Let's get percussive! Chopping is a sound you can make with your bow. It doesn't sound like any particular note, because the bow moves a little bit along the string, instead of across it like normal.

There are two ways to chop. One way has the bow hairs pointed away from you, towards the scroll. The other way has the bow hairs pointed toward you and the bridge. Either way, your thumb needs to hold the bow on the stick rather than under the frog. The hairs will be tilted instead of coming straight down, but this will happen with enough force that all the hairs will end up on the string.

To chop, hold your bow an inch or two above the strings. Move the bow REALLY fast down onto the strings, using your arm (rather than your fingers or wrist). Let the weight of your arm sink into the string. The bow should move along the string, not in the direction of a down bow. It should make a crunching sound, and the bow should come to a complete stop in the string.

Once the bow has stopped moving, you can pick up your bow and try it again.

Be sure to stay right at the frog (where the hair is tight), but be careful not to hit the metal part of the bow on your strings or on the body of your instrument!

Once you can make a chopping sound, try to alternate it with some chord notes. Let's try "D." (Remember, we can use our D and A strings at the same time when we see "D.")

Don't pick up the bow after the chop. Leave it on the string and pull the chord notes from there. Let the open strings ring as your bow is in the air getting ready to chop again. The chords are not played using a long bow, but are more like a pizzicato with your bow.

Once you can alternate ringing the strings with chopping, try it with "Soldier's Joy." (Don't worry about the A7 for now — we'll cover that in later books.) Once you've learned "Love Somebody," you can try that one as well.

Variation: Set Chop/Soft Chop

Once the tune gets to be too fast for the Circle Chop, try this instead! Simply set your bow on the string in between chops, in rhythm, instead of playing the chord.

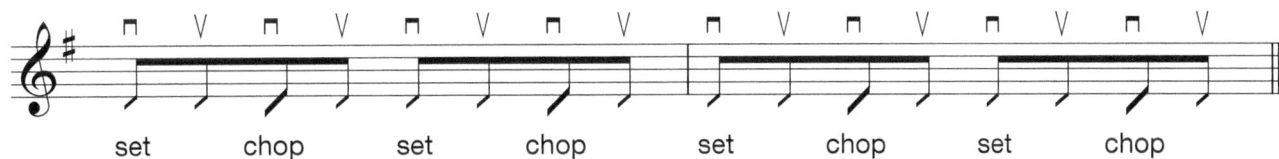

You can even create a variation in which you use both Circle Chop and Set Chop in one bar.

Try it, it sounds really cool!

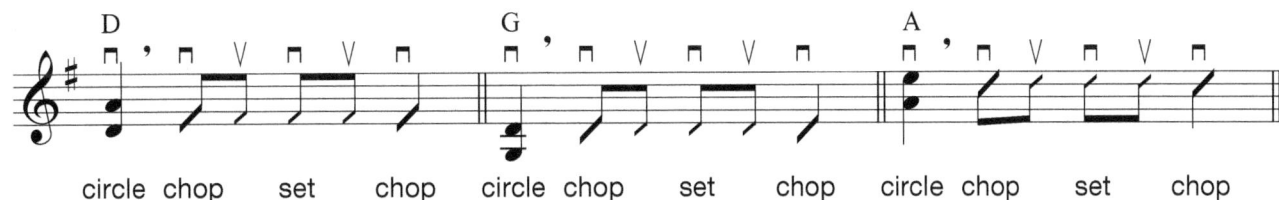

Be sure to see *AltStrings.com* for video lessons on these accompaniments!

Here are some tunes to practice your hooked bow (two down bows or two up bows in a row).

Row Your Boat

* Second player starts when first player gets here for a round.

Pop Goes the Weasel

Off She Goes

History

Fiddlers may have played this tune when a ship left the harbor.

Performance Notes

This tune is a great chance to practice your hooked bowing. Note that these have lines instead of dotes, which means you should make the hooked bows smoother, for a more singing line.

altstrings.com/
violin-fiddle-bk1-18

altstrings.com/
violin-fiddle-bk1-19

altstrings.com/
violin-fiddle-bk1-20

Playing in a Band

So you want to play in an existing band or put one together with your friends? Great! Here are some tips:

Usually, bands have at least one each of the following members:

- Someone whose primary job is to play the melody, and be the "face" of the ensemble
- Someone whose primary job is to play the chords
- Some type of bass player — this can be the same as the chord player

Other jobs in a band:

- Someone has to be the speaker during concerts; someone who communicates with the audience, like the narrator of the concert. This job can be passed around between band members, but usually it's primarily one person.
- Every band needs a manager, or someone to: handle booking performances, schedule and run rehearsals, and promote the band's concerts. These jobs can of course be divided among band members (or even people outside the band).

Now, on to the music!

Intros: The tune has to start somehow! Some common ways to start a tune are:

- Play "potatoes" or a count off, using the rhythm of "Twinkle, Twinkle Little Star" in *Book 1* (see the "Twinkle" lesson at *AltStrings.com* for how to add this type of introduction to a tune.)
- Play part of the tune, usually that last couple of bars, before the tune starts
- Just jump right in at the beginning of the tune!
- It works well to have one person, several people or everyone play the intro

Melody: If you know the tune, you can always play the tune! Sometimes it's nice to let one person play the tune solo with only one or two people playing the chords. If there are usually a lot of people playing the melody, this can be a nice change in sound. This is true in a jam session, too!

Chords: If you are the person playing the chords, it works well to play different rhythmic patterns over the chords each time through the tune. See the videos at *AltStrings.com* for ideas on how to accompany tunes!

Harmony: In *Book 2*, we will learn how to create harmonies using only the melody and chord symbols. It works well to play only the tune one time through, then add one or two harmony parts the second time through.

Endings: There are several ways to end a tune, and choosing different endings for different tunes makes things more interesting for the audience.

- Short stop: play the tune and simply stop short on the last note. This is a very exciting way to end a tune!
- Long ending: play the tune as normal, but extend the length of the last note.
- Variation: change the notes in the last measure or so of music to a more exciting, final-sounding ending. This is your chance to compose!
- Tag: end the tune, then add a little melody to the end (see "Twinkle, Twinkle Little Star" in *Book 1* for an example.) This is most often done in American music like Old-Time and Bluegrass.

Creating a set: Since fiddle tunes are so short, most of the time you'll want to play a tune more than once. You'll also want to play more than one tune in a row.

- When choosing tunes to play in a set together for performance, it makes the most sense to choose to use tunes that come from the same region. You may also want to put tunes of different speeds in order from slowest to fastest; for example if you're playing a Scottish set, you could play a march, then a strathspey, then reels.

- You can learn a lot by listening to how other fiddlers put their sets together.

- When arranging sets for a concert, you'll want to alternate playing fast sets with slow tunes. You usually want to start and end halves of the concert with fast tunes, and play about twice as many fast or medium-speed sets as you do slow tunes.

Tips for Jamming

- If you've been invited to lead a tune, pick one you know really well, and play it at least twice in a row so that others can join in.

- Unless you've been invited to lead a tune, it's best not to play louder than anyone else.

- It's great to try and figure out a tune by ear during a jam! That way you can learn it and join in next time you come. Be sure to ask the name of a tune you'd like to learn to make it easier to find later. You may even ask someone if you can record them playing the tune slowly for you, so that you can learn their version at home and play it with them next time.

- Before the tune starts, ask what key the tune is in. That way you can figure out which chord will be the most common. By playing the chords, you can play along with a tune you don't know.

- If someone is singing a song or playing a tune by themselves and most other people aren't playing too, it's most polite just to listen to their solo, rather than make too much noise trying to figure it out on your instrument.

- Have fun!

Check out our other books in the *AltStrings Fiddle Method* series:

Books 3 and *4* build on your exciting skills, using lots of transcriptions of real recordings by today's great fiddlers!

Continue your study of playing accompaniment with chords, creating harmonies, and adding traditional ornamentation, by seeing for yourself how the masters do it!

Our series for other instruments includes *AltStrings Fiddle Method* books for Violin, Viola and Bass.

Audio recordings and play-along backing tracks are available through iTunes, as well as at *AltStrings.com*.

Check out *AltStrings.com* for sheet music arrangements of traditional, folk, pop, rock, jazz and holiday music, for over 20 types of bowed string ensemble!

Happy Fiddling!

Acknowledgements

A big THANK YOU to the many music teachers who have shared their talent and wisdom with me over the years, especially Kathleen Spring, my Suzuki violin teacher trainer, and Bobbi Nikles, my mentor and editor, both of whom have always been so generous with their time. Thanks to my friends Kim Bird, Evan Shelton, and Meaghan Salton, for their cello and bass expertise. Thanks to Charylu Roberts for her wonderful layout work, as well as for teaching me about the publishing industry, and being the reliable sounding board I need for all my crazy ideas. I love working with you! Thanks to Mary McMurtry and Jess Blackburn; your work is beautiful! Thanks of course to my Nicola; you are my reason. Thanks also to my family, who have by now hopefully given up on the idea that I might be a veterinarian someday.

www.ingramcontent.com/pod-product-compliance
Lightning Source LLC
LaVergne TN
LVHW081337060426
835513LV00014B/1331